INTENTION

Disclaimer:

This book is not intended to replace expert advice from professional practiioners. It is intended for informational purposes only. The author and the publisher are not medical practitioners nor counsellors, and professional advice should be sought before embarking on any programme discussed in the book. Welbeck Publishing Group and the author make no representations or warranties of any kind, express or implied, and specifically disclaims, to the extent permitted by law, any implied warranties of merchantability or fitness for a particular purpose and any injury, illness, damage, death, liability or loss incurred, directly or indirectly from the use or application of any of the information contained in this book.

Published in 2023 by Welbeck
An imprint of Welbeck Non-Fiction Limited
part of Welbeck Publishing Group
Offices in: London – 20 Mortimer Street, London W1T 3JW &
Sydney – Level 17, 207 Kent St, Sydney NSW 2000 Australia
www.welbeckpublishing.com

Text © Dani Sullivan 2023
Design and layout © Welbeck Non-fiction Limited 2023

ISBN 978-1-80279-601-8

Printed in China

10 9 8 7 6 5 4 3 2 1

MIX
Paper | Supporting
responsible forestry
FSC® C020056

INTENTION

10 WAYS TO MANIFEST A MORE PURPOSEFUL LIFE

DANI SULLIVAN, LCSW

WELBECK

CONTENTS

MEET THE AUTHOR

Hi there, my name is Dani Sullivan, LCSW. I am a non-binary and neurodivergent human practicing embodiment and connection as a clinical social worker, therapist and educator. I am the founder of Intentions Therapy, a small clinical practice offering individual, group and relationship healing in the United States, based in South Florida. Discernment of our purpose is the first step to living with intention and a big part of therapy. This is why my therapeutic practice is called Intentions Therapy.

I am passionate about embracing self-acceptance and attuning to the most vulnerable parts of self with radical compassion, non-judgement and dignity. My roots as a social worker are in storytelling, community organizing, and restorative justice and I am passionate about teaching self-healing and relationship-healing for collective well-being. My work seeks to challenge narratives of division, separation, fear and hopelessness by holding space for people to embrace the fullness of their identity, expression and experience. I teach folks from all walks of life to slow down, listen inwards, meet their body, and clarify a healing path through whatever stands in their way. This process can be summed up by the phrase "living with intention". Intentional living feels aligned, attuned, and grounded in the truth of our needs, ambitions, limitations, and circumstances.

My core values are diversity, self-respect, and dignified connection. I pull heavily from the Neuro-Affective Relational Model, Somatic Mindfulness and Identity-Based Healing through the lens of intersectional feminism, embodiment and collective liberation. The intention behind this text is to make my favourite parts of therapy easier to access. We all need resources to support us in accessing nourishment, ease, connection and healing, but these services can be expensive, inaccessible or even impossible for many people and for many reasons. Every human is worthy and deserving of individualized care, time and space to discern their path, so I am here to teach individuals to offer this care, time and space to themselves.

This text will offer anyone struggling with feeling lost, unclear or disconnected from their purpose to set clear, heartfelt intentions and step into new ways of being. With interactive exercises and accessible techniques that you can implement right away, readers will be invited to restore their relationship with their inner being and shed patterns of fear, denial, shame and disconnection. Letting go of the subconscious beliefs that keep us stuck in survival mode allows fertile space for us to plant seeds of hope, community and worthiness.

SELF-HEALING FOR COLLECTIVE CARE

Dear Reader,

Are you looking for healing? You must be if you picked up this book, or someone must be looking out for you.

Most people looking to clarify their intentions are seeking healing. And if you have made it here, you will know this is an invitation from the author to work on yourself for the betterment of us all. This is not a punishment, but an invitation sent to you through this text to clarify your intentions and heal yourself. "Working on yourself" is hard and it is a lifelong process. Living with intention is a possibility for anyone looking to commit to this process and to a lifetime of practice.

I only want you to continue reading if you want to work on yourself. If that is something you are disinterested in, this book is not for you. Invitations are just that – a choice: you can respond to this invitation however you want. You don't need a sure-fire "yes" nor a solid "no". You can fall anywhere on the spectrum of "yes" and "no". All you need to continue forwards in this text is a willingness to listen inwards.

Consider the words you read here, enough to hear your own inner voice.

The rest is about moving inwards for clarity.

ARE YOU LOOKING FOR HEALING?

Clarifying intention, focusing on hope and moving through our environments with purpose is a way we can heal ourselves. As a clinical social worker and therapist, I see the ways that individual healing has a ripple effect on families, partnerships and the world around us.

Learning to live with intention requires connecting with yourself: your truth, your needs, your experiences and your heart. And for so many, that can be scary. But fear not: the same way you can learn a skill like cooking or riding a bike, you can learn to connect with your desires and know yourself. This work will scaffold upon simple tools you already have but might just need practice with, like slowing down, using your senses and listening inwards.

These skills of self-knowing and of social and emotional wellness are so frequently left off the school curriculum that many of us lack basic emotional education. Concepts like self-regulation, mindfulness, reflection and rest have not been embedded into academic and social curriculum. This is one of the ways that we systematically fail young folks, especially those on the margins with legacies of intergenerational trauma.

It is my hope that this text provides easily accessible tools for people of all walks of life and all different genders, bodies, races and lived experiences. Thank you for being here and thank you for turning inwards to clarify your intentions.

If you are still trying to figure out...

- How to care for yourselves

- How to process and understand your experiences

- How to listen inwards for long enough to know what it is you truly want

- How to understand your needs and limitations

- How to act with intention

This is the education you can expect from this book: accessible practices and guided exercises that you can learn, share and repeat to centre your life with truth and intention.

Through this book, I hope to offer some version of self-healing. I frequently define my own role as a therapist as an "educator of self-healing". I am not an expert on anyone's life but my own. I am not a healer outside of my own self-healing. I am not changing the world for myself, I am changing my relationship with myself and letting my relationships in the world do the work.

So, lovely reader, you are the expert on your own life. You are in the driver's seat. You are an agent of positive change, if you would like to be. Take whatever resonates within the following pages and leave the rest.

Give yourself permission to make mistakes, have fun, explore and play with the different experiences and guided practices that follow. After all, most experiences, even uncomfortable ones, have something to teach us.

YOU ARE IN THE

DRIVER'S SEAT

Isn't it a joy to be able to choose our own challenges?

Take care, and set abundant intentions.

In solidarity,

Dani Sullivan, LCSW (They/Them)

WHAT IS SELF-HEALING?

Healing of the self means healing of the whole person. No part of you can be left behind. Self-healing is intersectional and integrative. Self-healing is a generative practice of working with our energy and our relationship with our personhood. Self-healing is a lifelong practice of caring for our body, our needs, our relationships and our world. This is an inherently spiritual practice of clarifying our deepest intentions for our life. Self-healing requires living relationships and true self care.

WHAT IS COLLECTIVE CARE?

Essentially, collective care is caring for and about the collective. The collective is the general experience of all of humanity. When you consider a collective, it is a union across division. Unions and relationships can grow in even the most hostile environments. Collectives of care are systems are that interwoven around concepts of care for the humans around us, the spirit within us, and our cultural and interpersonal well-being.

Reflection is the language of hope. Use this book as a space to reflect, consider, process, daydream, set intentions and connect with self.

Each chapter includes guided practices, activity suggestions, and space for reflection and journaling. Don't worry about spelling, or grammar. Write for yourself. This book is for you. Allow yourself to be messy here, allow yourself to be yourself here.

There is no right or wrong way to use this book.

REFLECTION IS THE LANGUAGE OF HOPE

WHAT ARE YOU NEEDING THE MOST FROM INTENTION?

JOURNAL EXERCISE

• What brought you here to begin engaging with this book? Why now? Are you looking for healing? If so, from what?

....
....
....
....

• What are you needing the most from your journey with Intention?

....
....
....
....
....

• If you were 10 per cent more connected to and aligned with yourself, what do you hope will be different in your life?

....
....
....
....
....

A NOTE ON DIVERSITY AND RELATIONSHIPS

Diversity is a natural part of being human. We are very different, and we are here together. Our diversity is our strength. Finding ways to relate across our differences is key to the success of humanity.

Being in a relationship with one another is a practice of trust.

We must embody the idea that no one is disposable. That we are here for one another. I believe that any person is capable of finding wellness and wholeness for themselves when given the freedom to self-determine and the resources for healing. This book strives to make intentional living accessible to all people, regardless of age, religion, race, class, gender, sexual orientation, ability, legal status, immigration status, physical appearance or national origin.

Healing work requires us to consider the needs of people in marginalized bodies and identities. I do this by celebrating neurodiversity, taking pride in queer and trans experiences, amplifying the voices of black and brown creators (see the Further Reading List for some suggestions) and focusing on highlighting the intersection of beauty and complexity. We must unlearn internalized oppression in order to find freedom to live out our intentions. As a therapist and clinical social worker, I practice from a non-pathologizing perspective. This means that I do not view groups of symptoms, behaviours, conditions and experiences as inherently abnormal, unhealthy and disordered. There is no inherent wrong or bad, just natural diversity. I see the full spectrum of humanity and we are as diverse, complex and abundantly creative as the natural world we come from. There is a world outside of you and a world inside of you that are here to be explored. These worlds hold an immense, interconnected network of diverse relationships and entangled energy. This complex entanglement fills our world with a rainbow of colours. Human diversity is a spectrum of experience.

I hope to interrupt systems of oppression by pushing back against the belief that there is anything "wrong", disordered or problematic with a liberated, embodied, fully expressive human experience. There is no right or wrong way to be a human, just your way. Intentional living requires you to be exactly who you are. You don't need to change to fit into the world around you. You belong here just because you exist. We are in desperate need of your uniqueness. Don't forget how much you matter.

You are deeply deserving of a liberated, embodied, expressive experience if you would like it – we all are.

INTENTIONS 101 & VALUES BASED LIVING

WHAT IS AN INTENTION?

An intention is what we want the most, what our heart would ask for if it could speak. The origin of the word "intention" comes from the verb "intend":

Intend (verb)

From the Latin *intendere* with root words in "inwards" and *ten* "towards"; *intendere* means to "turn one's attention", "to strain in quest" and "to stretch out, extend towards".

To "intend" is to move both inwards and towards. To intend is to turn one's attention inwards, to bring clarity to one's focus, to listen in quest of something.

Intention (noun)

From the Latin *intensio*, "a stretching, exertion" or "effort to stretch outwards". From the Latin *intensionem*, "the action of stretching and straining towards".

An intention is a will, a wish, a purpose, or an aim. An intention is a movement towards something from our centre. Intentions come from inside us and they direct us forward in quest of what we want.

A WILL, A WISH, A PURPOSE OR AN AIM

SEVEN STEPS TOWARDS INTENTIONAL LIVING:

1 Be present. Notice what it's like to be alive.

2 Slow down. Pause. Be quiet.

3 In silence, listen inwardly.

4 Imagine what you want.

5 Stretch towards the centre of your desires by asking "why?"

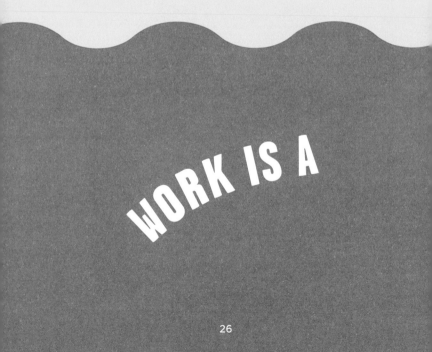

WORK IS A

REALITY OF LIFE

6 Clarify what you intend. Bring your attention inward and toward your intention.

7 Act in accordance with your intention.

Intention-setting is simple, intentional living is a bit more complicated.

You must work towards your intentions. Work is a reality of life – you don't get what you want without moving towards it. Follow these steps to live with intention and repeat daily.

THE INNER COMPASS

Your inner being is carrying a compass. This compass is simple: it acts like any old compass, it helps you to position yourself and locate where you are. Traditional compasses provide a sense of direction as we navigate through the Earth's terrain. Your inner compass offers direction as you navigate your life.

On any journey you take, it is likely you will lose your way. When trying to find your way home, you must stop, pause at your current location and hold your compass level to get a sense of direction. Then you must use a map or any reference materials you have to geolocate yourself.

When we pause, we have time to rest. Rest is anything that connects our mind and body. In rest, we can look inwards and imagine our intentions. Tricia Hersey speaks of Rest as Resistance and imagination in her manifesto, which is included in the Further Reading list (page 190). Intention setting doesn't happen without slowing down. You can't read your inner compass without pausing.

The same way as the Earth has a natural geomagnetic field, we have our own field of inner energy. The Earth has a North and a South Pole. These opposite poles attract, they hold the Earth together. This geomagnetic field is one of the invisible forces holding our world together.

The magnetic needle in a traditional compass is suspended in liquid and responds to our movement and location as we travel. When we hold our compass level and pause to geolocate, we can identify the "magnetic north".

The magnetic North Pole of Earth does not match up perfectly with our geographic North Pole, or what we call "true north". The magnetic north is not stable or fixed, our northernmost magnetic point is always changing. What we know to be "north" moves around as our planet's magnetic field warps over time. Some estimate that in the last century, the magnetic North Pole has moved nearly 965 kilometres (600 miles) towards Siberia. What beautiful, natural evidence of change.

I like to remember I am from this Earth. I am a part of nature, a form of complex life on planet Earth.

We all are, essentially, nature. So, in the same way the Earth has direction, energy and change, so too does my life.

To use a compass, you have to look up, down and all around to orient yourself to your world and environment. Knowing which direction is North and South is our map to returning home. Our inner compass is responding not to the North and South magnetic Poles but to our own perception of good and bad, right and wrong.

The needle in our compass points to our truth and our deepest values. The inner compass is a tool that truth seekers can use to find the light. We can use our inner compass to find our way home. We are here living, walking one another home.

The truth is something we can orient towards, reference and integrate, but we never get to "the pure, full truth". This is because the truth is always changing.

The truth is complex and intersectional. Finding the truth is an individual and personal practice as much as it is a collective and communal need. Truth seeking isn't about the destination. You don't ever "get there" as long as you're alive, you just learn more about what is true for you.

WHY SET INTENTIONS?

Intentions help us to read our inner compass. Essentially, they help us to define our truth.

Setting intentions is about aiming towards what you want for yourself. Without them, we can feel aimless, unsure of what we care about, or lacking in passion, resolve and will. Many feel lost, lonely, disconnected and unfocused.

Are you wandering around without aim?

When using a bow and arrow, you must pause first to focus on your target. Before you aim, you pull back on the bow, moving inwards. This inward movement is necessary for your arrow to fly with force towards its target.

If you want to reach your goals, you are going to have to look inside yourself. Try setting some intentions...

ARE YOU WANDERING AROUND WITHOUT AIM?

WHAT WE WANT
+ WHAT WE NEED
+ WHAT DO

INTENTION SETTING FORMULA: WHAT WE WANT + WHAT WE NEED + WHAT WE ARE DO

Ask yourself:

1   What do I want for myself?

....
....
....
....

2   What do I need to survive?

....
....
....
....

3   How can I move forward with my needs and desires in focus?

....
....
....
....

SET CLEAR INTENTIONS

An intention is a purpose, a mission statement, the "why" behind whatever we are doing. We all have the capacity to live our truth with intention.

Intention setting happens in the present. You can set intentions for everything and anything. You can clarify your intentions for the day, your work, a yoga class, your relationships with family and friends, even your next trip to the store. Intentions help us to aim in the right direction as we live our daily lives.

Intentions are deeply personal, there are no universal intentions. They are unique to each individual person – we all have different prayers and desires, and requests of life.

Consider what needs to be healed in your life and clarify your intention with these questions:

1 If you could change one thing about the world to make your existence more joyful, expansive, creative and lovely, what would you want to change?

....
....

INTENTION SETTING HAPPENS IN THE PRESENT

2 What do you need in the present season of your life? How can you focus on your needs in a way that generates solutions?

....

....

3 If you had a magic wand and could ask for anything in the world, what would you want? How would you show up for your life if your wish came true?

INTENTION

CLARIFICATION

How would you feel? What would you share?

....

....

4 Set an intention for your journey with this book.
   What do you want for yourself out of this guided
   experience?

....

....

FOCUS – A LOST ART

"What should we focus on?"

This question causes many of my clients to squirm in their seats. Why? It gets straight to the heart of whatever they are needing help with. They're not able to small talk or distract from what they need. Identifying a focus bypasses distractions and asks us to identify the heart of the matter. Focus is a necessity to get anything done with intentionality.

In this day and age, concentration has become a lost art. The amount of noise in our world is increasing as our technology and devices become more saturated with content and more difficult to put down. Distraction abounds. If you are easily distracted, forgetful and struggle with concentration, know you are in good company. Focus can be cultivated through practice and our experience of the world will shift if we learn to focus on what matters to us.

WHAT WE FOCUS ON EXPANDS

If you dedicated one hour per week to heal something, what would you focus on?

Intention setting requires us to have a positive focus on what we want, not what we lack. For example, "I don't want to fail this test" is a worry (or a prayer for what we don't want), whereas "I am smart and capable of acing this test" is an intention set with positivity.

Ask yourself:

• What does abundance look like for me?

• What practices help me to feel most connected to meaning?

• How do I define success?

• What brings me joy?

Complete these sentences:

I want more of this in my life: _____, _____ and _____.

I would like my life to be _____ and _____.

FEEL YOUR BODY

SIMPLE PRACTICES TO CULTIVATE FOCUS AND ENHANCE CONCENTRATION

1 **Mindful Breathing** Take ten full, deep breaths. Inhale through your nose and exhale slowly from your mouth. Notice the pause between your inhales and exhales. Feel your body.

2 **Embodied Relaxation** Feel your body as you breathe deeply. Bring your attention to where your body is carrying tension. Take a moment to intentionally relax those areas of the body, sending breath and presence to the body's most tense and tender areas. Or find a guided "Progressive Muscle Relaxation" online.

3 **Candle Meditation** One of my favourite Ayurvedic practices that helps with concentration, this can be done with a lit candle or by visualizing a candle or inner light. Focus your gaze and attention on the source of light and follow the movements of the flame with your eyes. Breathe deeply and relax. Allow whatever thoughts and feelings arise to melt into the flame. Start with one minute and increase from there. Finish your meditation by closing your eyes, rubbing your hands together, cupping your palms over your eyes and offering yourself gratitude for practicing. Bring your hands to your heart and visualize the light source in your heart space. When complete, blow out your candle.

VALUES-BASED LIVING

Our values help us find our way through the dark. They are what our heart holds closest and what is most valuable to our inner being. Our values can be our guideposts as we navigate choices and changes in our life. They help us to know where we stand in relation to others, ourselves and the world.

Checking in with your values is a sure-fire way to clarify your intentions and get a level read on your inner compass. The value clarification is an opportunity to reflect on what is most important to us.

VALUE CLARIFICATION

As you read through the list of values on the next few pages, mark between 10 and 20 values that speak to you.

This list of values builds upon Brené Brown's work in *Dare to Lead* and you can find more of her work in the Further Reading list, page 190.

LIST OF VALUES

Accountability
Achievement
Activism
Adaptability
Adventure
Affirmation
Agency
Ambition
Ancestry
Authenticity
Balance
Beauty
Belonging
Career
Caring
Co-creation
Collaboration
Commitment
Community
Compassion
Competence
Competition
Confidence
Connection
Contentment
Contribution
Cooperation
Courage
Creativity
Curiosity

Dignity
Diversity
Efficiency
Environment
Equality
Ethics
Excellence
Fairness
Faith
Family
Forgiveness
Freedom
Friendship
Fun
Future
Generations
Generosity
Grace
Gratitude
Grief
Growth
Harmony
Health
Heritage
Home
Honesty
Hope
Humility
Humour
Inclusion

Independence
Initiative
Integrity
Intersectionality
Intuition
Joy
Justice
Kindness
Knowledge
Leadership
Learning
Legacy
Leisure
Liberty
Listening
Love
Loyalty
Nature
Openness
Optimism
Order
Parenting
Patience
Peace
Perseverance
Personal
fulfilment
Power
Pride
Recognition

OUR VALUES BECOME GUIDEPOSTS FOR LIFE'S CHOICES AND CHANGES

Reliability	Serenity	Tradition
Repair	Service	Travel
Representation	Simplicity	Trust
Resourcefulness	Sovereignty	Truth
Respect	Solitude	Understanding
Responsibility	Spirituality	Uniqueness
Rest	Stability	Usefulness
Risk-taking	Stewardship	Vision
Security	Success	Vulnerability
Self-discipline	Sustainability	Wealth
Self-expression	Teamwork	Well-being
Self-respect	Thrift	Wholeness
Sensitivity	Time	Wisdom

Add in your own values:

....

....

....

....

Write the values that speak to you the most in the box below.

Now group similar values into boxes:

Now identify your top three values:

Value one: ....

Value two:..

Value three: ....

ALIGNING YOUR VALUES WITH YOUR LIFESTYLE

1. What does it feel like to be aligned with this value?

Value one: ....

Value two: ....

Value three: ....

2. What actions support the growth of this value?

Value one: ....

Value two: ....

Value three: ....

3. What people, places, and routines support me to live this value?

Value one: ....

Value two: ....

Value three: ....

PERSONAL NEEDS AND LIFE PURPOSE

ATTUNE TO YOUR NEEDS

SELF-ATTUNEMENT — KNOWING WHAT YOU NEED

Many humans feel disconnected from a knowledge of their needs. We have a hard time feeling into our bodies, our individual and collective experience, and putting words to what we are lacking and what might help. For many of us, this difficulty in knowing our needs results from a lack of attunement early in life. Without a loving witness, many of us did not have room to explore our experience, speak about our desires and find language for our pain.

Attunement is our capacity to be present with and a witness to expressions of experience in ourselves and others. It moves beyond empathy to recognize, understand and relationally respond to the legitimate needs and pain one witnesses in ourselves and others.

Attunement...

• Can be achieved by yourself and in relationships

• Feels like a warm embrace when you're in pain

• Allows your needs to be seen and heard

• Provides regulation and soothing for the nervous system

- Involves authentic and vulnerable communication with self and other

- Creates emotional safety and security

- Soothes pain in a way that is manageable and regulating

- Allows us to exist in connection with ourselves and the world around us

Attunement is what therapy and healing are all about – learning that we can feel safe to rest, digest and exist in connection with ourselves and others, knowing

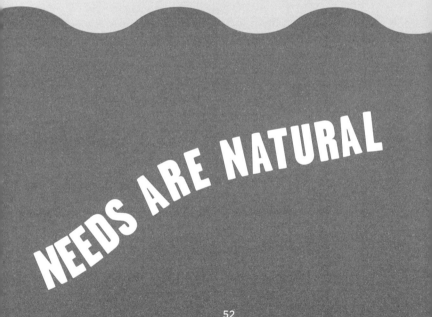

NEEDS ARE NATURAL

AND EVOLVING

that whatever experiences and needs arise in the present moment will be met with understanding, non-judgement and care.

Self-Attunement is simple: knowing what you need. Needs are natural and evolving. You might not need something now, but as conditions of your life change, new needs emerge. By checking in with yourself and identifying your needs frequently, you can practice self-attunement with ease.

One of my favourite self-attunement practices is a Needs Assessment.

NEEDS ASSESSMENT EXERCISE

- **Body Needs** Feel into your body. To do this, turn down the volume of your thoughts and drop into your sensory experience. Notice where your body is carrying pain, stress or tension. Assess for any needs that would increase your comfort and embodied presence. What does your body need? Does it need rest, nourishment, movement or touch?

....

....

- **Safety Needs** What do you need to feel safe and secure? Do you need community or a safe environment, protection from harm or legal rights and protections?

....

....

- **Individual Needs** Reflect on your personal experience as an individual. What do you need to feel secure in your sense of self? Do you need independence, self-acceptance, meaning, respect or space to explore your curiosity and expression?

....

....

- **Relationship Needs** Notice where your relationships could use tending by identifying your relationship needs. What social or relationship needs would support your capacity for connection? Do your relationships need more understanding, reciprocity, attunement, trust or friendship?

....
....

- **Spiritual Needs** Check in with your heart to identify what might help you feel aligned in the present. What does your spirit need to feel alive? Are you seeking hope, pleasure, peace, beauty or a space to grieve or practice spirituality?

....
....

Finish your needs assessment by thanking yourself for taking the time to enquire into your needs and tune inwards.

Closing Statement: "I honour all that I hold and embody today. I trust myself to take care of my body, mind, spirit and relationships as my needs arise. I am witnessing myself without judgement and in loving awareness. I am grateful for my needs – they show me I am alive."

Body Needs

Water

Food

Health

Air

Rest

Shelter

Pleasure

Fresh Air

Space

Stimulation

Movement

Comfort

Touch

Sleep

Warmth

Rejuvenation

Sexual Expression

Nurturing

Relief

Choice

Autonomy

Healthcare

Safety Needs

Stability

Consistency

Support

Order/Structure

Peaceful Environments

Security of Mind and Body

Peace of Mind

Trust

Financial Security

Security of Resources

Access to Health and Wellness

Time

Safe Community

Protection from Harm

Legal Rights and Protections

Freedom from Danger

Physical Safety

Emotional Safety

Safe Space for Emotional Expression

Relationship Needs

Connection
Appreciation
Companionship
Support
Affirming Community
Empathy
Kindness
Communication
Honesty
Mutual Recognition
Attunement
Love
Partnership
Belonging
Trust
Friendship
Intimacy
Reciprocity
Understanding Others
Equity

Respect
Giving Affection
Receiving Affection
Secure Emotional Connection
To Be heard, Seen
To be Known, Understood
To be Trusted
Inclusion
Participation
Closeness
Harmony
Sharing

Spiritual Needs

Hope
Joy
Creativity
Mattering to Myself
Play
Inspiration
Purpose
Will
Mourning/Grief
Service
Contribution
Celebration
Faith
Beauty
Spiritual Practice
Prayer
Consciousness
Interconnectedness
Flow
Presence
Alignment
Inner Peace
Vitality

Individual Needs

Presence

Meaning

Self-Care

Self-Compassion

Awareness

Respect

Healing

Consideration

Freedom

Integrity

Autonomy

Focus

Independence

Self-Love

Authenticity

Self-Regulation

Consistency

Clarity

Motivation

Self-Expression

Self-Responsibility

Curiosity

Ease

Tenderness

Dignity

Self-Acceptance

Self-Knowledge

Growth

Exploration

Discovery

To access the full printable list of human needs and a guided version of this needs assessment exercise, visit intentionstherapy.com/needs

LIVING BOUNDARIES

There is no amount of healing that will keep you from having needs or requiring accommodation. Learning to speak the language of our needs is how we set boundaries. Living and changing boundaries are adaptive and necessary components of self-care.

Energy is the currency of life. Life is the spending and replenishing of energy. In reality, we all have limited energy. Our limitations and needs inform our boundaries. Boundaries allow us to love and care for ourselves while existing in relationships with others and the world.

True self-care interrupts the shame we may carry around having needs. Boundaries are shameless. Boundaries require we speak about our needs with love.

Boundaries communicate what you will allow or tolerate in your life. They can help you to establish free time, balance, trust and self-worth. The maintenance of personal boundaries insists we live in radical acceptance of our reality. Boundaries require honesty with ourself and those with whom we share relationships.

Boundary check-ins are the most powerful weapon you have to know your heart and change your life. I wish I could tell you that I meet all my clients' needs, that our weekly check-ins change the fabric of their lives. But this is so far from the reality and the truth that my clients are complex and diverse individuals with living and emerging needs; I meet almost none of them. It's not my job to meet their needs; it's my job to listen intently to their desires and to support them in meeting their own needs.

There is no way we can meet all of our needs all of the time. There are delays and obstacles to satisfying our needs. These unmet needs, and the legitimate obstacles and delayed gratification, are a reality of life.

Many clients struggle with therapy at the start because they are bringing awareness to the unmet needs in their lives. We are talking about the issues, the stuck parts and the pain. Unmet needs are uncomfortable, they affect us – it wouldn't be a need if it didn't cause us to shift and move towards it.

Intentional check-ins with self are necessary regardless of whether or not we can meet our needs immediately.

Very frequently, there is ongoing work and effort that must go into accommodating our needs as they emerge in the landscape of our lives. This labour is a reality. It can be done by us, or it must be built into our environment by someone else. This happens on every scale.

WHAT PURPOSE MOVES YOU?

LIFE PURPOSE CLARIFICATION

1   What do you need to thrive?

....

....

....

....

....

2   What are you most passionate about?

....

....

....

....

....

3   What talents, skills or abilities come most naturally
    to you?

....

....

....

....

....

INTENTION CLARIFICATION EXERCISE

Check in and set intentions with a clear focus on your needs and purpose.

Focus What do I want more of in my life? What positive changes can I focus on to welcome more success, joy, connection and abundance into my life?

Needs What are you in need of that you haven't been able to receive or give to yourself? (Use the lists on pages 56-59 as a word bank).

YOUR NEEDS

Goals What are you hoping to learn or understand about yourself or the mysteries of your life through this experience?

Drive What motivates you to set these intentions? What impact do you hope this work will have on you?

Find a printable intention clarification worksheet at intentionstherapy.com/print

BUILDING A FLEXIBLE DAILY PRACTICE

Your daily practice will change throughout the seasons of your life. In order to optimally respect your body as the vessel that allows you to experience life, you must be tuned into your body's experience. In a world that is always asking us to push a little harder and to labour despite our body's need for rest, daily check-ins with yourself are a necessity to survive and thrive.

FOUR ELEMENTS OF A DAILY PRACTICE

1 Feel your body

2 Focus inwards

3 Assess for needs

4 Set intentions

All of these items incorporate mindfulness and require that you notice how you feel and what you need throughout the day.

Meditation looks different for everyone. It means paying attention to the present moment on purpose and can be breath-focused, guided or a practice like

DAILY CONNECTION WITH THE SELF IS A NECESSITY TO THRIVE

prayer or yoga. Many people mindfully exercise or drink a cup of coffee/tea in the morning. Find something easy and satisfying that you can do daily to turn inwards, feel your body and know your needs.

DAILY INTENTIONS

Name your intentions daily. Get into the habit of identifying the purpose behind where you are spending your energy. Recite these purposes "out loud" in your daily life. You may write a few separate purpose statements for your daily use.

The purpose behind my work

....

....

....

....

....

My intentions for my rest and leisure time

....

....

....

....

What I value and desire in my relationships

....

....

....

....

My intentions for myself

....

....

....

....

....

How I hope to spend each day

....

....

....

....

....

The final step to any daily practice: express gratitude
and a commitment to return.

TRUE
SELF CARE

SELF-CARE IS A BASIC HUMAN NEED

What is the first thing that comes to your mind when you think of self-care? I believe our self-care culture has strayed so far from the truth and is in desperate need of real, true healing. Our self-care and wellness culture, especially in the United States is deeply rooted in capitalism and a drive for profit. Even the words 'self-care' have become a buzzword lacking in clarity. We confuse self-care with polishing our exterior – face masks, fitness memberships, bath bombs, and spa days... Don't get me wrong, I love these activities, but they are missing the mark when it comes to caring for our whole self. It is one of the deepest intentions of my life that we all realize how essential it is that we care for ourselves. That we heal our own wounds. That we learn the delicate and lifelong art of self-care as a community. That we focus our care on our relationships with self and other. That we tend to ourselves reciprocally as we tend to our world. Self-care requires we focus on liberatory practices and remaining in reality, remaining in our bodies. Our well-being as humans is dependent on our ability to remain embodied.

Bubble baths and yoga memberships are a luxury. Self-care is not. Self-care is a necessity. It is a basic human need. The need for self-care is universal. You cannot dismiss self-care in the same way you dismiss your New Year's resolutions once February rolls around. We, as a culture, cannot afford to dismiss this type of care. Without care, there is immeasurable distress and suffering. With care, there is healing.

There is hope. There is fullness and expansiveness that comes only through care. Minority stress does real damage on our entire bodily system, especially our nervous system. Self-care is the work we invest into undoing the chronic stress we have learned in our society. Self-care is resting, trusting in our body, listening to the symptoms of distress, pain, fatigue, inflammation, and feeling. Self-care is returning to our bodies. Finding a home in our bodies, and meeting our inner being.

LIFE-GIVING LISTS

DAILY WAYS TO TAKE CARE OF MYSELF

These can be things like daily movement or exercise routines, rest practices, activities, rituals, and even supplements or medications that help you stay healthy.

• Physical

....

....

....

....

....

....

....

• Emotional

....
....
....
....
....
....

• Relational

....
....
....
....
....
....

• Spiritual

....
....
....
....
....
....

SELF-CARE MENU ACTIVITIES THAT HELP ME FEEL BETTER:

Make a "self-care menu" with activities you can choose from to help yourself feel better. Leave this menu somewhere you can see it – hang it on your fridge or wall. Turn to the menu of self-care activities whenever you feel lost and choose whatever activity feels best for your current situation.

Example activities: take a few deep breaths, stretch your body, listen to your favourite song or album, journal out your thoughts, take a walk outside and look for birds and wildlife, make a craft with whatever you have at home, cook your favourite recipe, read a chapter of a book, follow a guided meditation or yoga practice, take a nice bath or shower, drink a full glass of water, call someone you love.

....
....
....
....
....
....
....
....
....
....
....
....

MAKE A "SELF-CARE MENU" WITH ACTIVITIES TO HELP YOU FEEL BETTER

PEOPLE I CAN TALK TO ABOUT MY NEEDS AND MY PURPOSE:

Most of us need to grow this list, so keep an open mind when it comes to the connections that come your way and take note of folks you can trust.

....
....
....
....
....
....

SAFE PEOPLE

AND SPACES

SPACES I FEEL AFFIRMED AND SAFE TO EXPLORE MY VULNERABILITY:

Communities, local supportive businesses, online groups, places of prayer, and practices like therapy.

....
....
....
....
....
....

THINGS THAT MAKE ME LAUGH:

Anything! Memes, videos, books, movies, comics, pictures, memories.

....
....
....
....
....
....
....
....

WHY DO YOU LOVE YOUR LIFE?

REASONS I LOVE MY LIFE:

Include the reason and date – this list is ongoing.

....

....

....

....

....

....

....

....

....

....

....

....

....

....

....

....

....

....

....

....

....

DIVORCE YOURSELF FROM URGENCY

DAILY RHYTHM

If we are able to harness a flexible daily practice of checking in with our needs and desires, we can find happiness and harmony within ourselves. There is a flow to life and a rhythm to our day-to-day happenings. Each day is a new opportunity to find balance in the rhythm of your life. Play with the speed of your day. Notice how you feel when you slow down and take breaks.

We each have our own unique pace and rhythm to our lives. I spent so many years judging myself because my timeline was different than those around me. I felt like I was growing up too fast, but also that I was behind on the learning curve. I still struggle with the sting of comparison, but now I focus more on the joy of moving at a pace that is right for me.

Divorce yourself from urgency. You don't need to get anywhere fast or learn in the blink of an eye. Take your time finding your way home. Learning is a life process. Let the rhythm of your work be dictated by your body and your heartfelt intentions. Urgency is a trauma response. Move slowly and find relief from the chronic stress you have endured. Life Medicine doesn't happen overnight, it happens over life.

SEASONS OF LIFE

There is an ebb and flow to the world around us and the world inside us. Life and death live alongside one another. There will be times of growth and play as well as times of loss and hibernation. I look to nature for support with big life changes. Nature helps me to accept what is. Nature allows me to access forgiveness. Nature is my safe space and connecting with the natural world around me is my deepest and most joyful spiritual practice.

The four seasons are a helpful framework to consider the ways your life is ebbing and flowing.

Spring: renewal and rejuvenation, fresh starts, growth and fertility, noticing beauty, freshness, grace and spirituality. Planting seeds and practicing hope.

Summer: optimism, positivity and hope for the future, connection and exploration, playfulness and openness to inspiration, cultivation of our passions, imagining endless possibilities.

Autumn: embracing change, transformation, culmination of projects, harvesting and celebrating our work and growth.

Winter: moving inward, reflection, review, and rest. Sensing and naming loss, shedding what no longer serves us, processing grief and letting go,

NATURE ALLOWS ME TO ACCESS FORGIVENESS

hibernating and slowing down, setting intentions for the next orbit around the sun.

Your emotional seasons may not always coincide with Earth's seasons. There is a time for everything, and everything comes in its own time. Trust that you are exactly where you need to be in your process, and be patient with yourself. If you have been in winter, know that spring will come soon.

THERE IS A TIME FOR EVERYTHING

JOURNAL EXERCISE

• What season are you in right now?

....
....

• How have you learned to deal with the ebb and
flow of your life? Where do you find rhythm and
harmony?

....
....

• How do you relate to the natural world around you?
Do changes to the weather and seasons of your
environment impact your lived experience?

....
....
....
....
....
....
....
....
....
....

HEALING OUTSIDE THE BINARY IS FOR EVERYONE (LITERALLY)

5

IDENTITY INFORMED HEALING

As a non-binary and neurodivergent therapist, my focus is on working alongside clients in cultivating acceptance, healing from complex trauma and reconciling the relationship with self. I support people in connecting to their truth, knowing their needs and desires, and aligning with personal values. I am a white, queer and non-binary trans person with chronic and invisible illness. Here, I want to share some of my own experience with identity-informed healing and living outside the gender binary.

Developmental and complex trauma are common for queer and trans individuals, and this endured trauma is compounded by intersecting experiences of disabilities, mental health concerns, racism, poverty and family. The same goes for me as a young girl, growing up in a Catholic family, parish and school system. My religious trauma was compounded by my queer sexuality, family trauma, severe anxiety and neurosensory processing sensitivities, and growing disconnect from my physical body due to chronic health issues, embodied pain and mental health crisis.

We know that healthy human development is impacted by environmental oppression. Minority stress is real and can be chronic. Because of this, queer and trans folks are often late bloomers, and many struggle with knowing their desires and true intentions. In my personal experience, I witness these developmental interruptions as delays in self-understanding, self-advocacy and authentic connection. My capacity to connect in healthy and safe ways to myself, my body and others were greatly impacted by internalized homophobia, transphobia, ableism and stigma.

Silencing and environmental mis-attunement are breeding grounds for shame, self-loathing, dissociation, dysphoria, and disembodiment. These are all symptoms of minority stress. That is why we must unlearn the core beliefs and survival strategies that keep us disempowered and feeling small, victimized, and stuck in despair. Intentional living requires we realign with our truth and values in the present; this is first and foremost in self-healing.

BLACK AND

WHITE THINKING

One of the most challenging, cognitive survival strategies that protected me the most as an at-risk queer youth was black and white thinking. It makes it much easier to cope with a cruel and complicated world if we can simplify it into "good" and "bad" categories. We become invested in the narrative that we only deserve self-compassion, dignity and grace if we are "good" or if we act, think, speak or exist in a certain way that we have either implicitly or explicitly learned is "good" or "right" in our world, through examples in the media, legal and school systems, cultural norms, religious teachings or family attitudes.

Divest from the narrative that there is a "good" and a "bad" way. Binaries like this don't allow space for growth, mistakes, change or complexity. Trying to fit yourself into a box labelled "good" will end up feeling like a cage so release yourself of this punishment. Contemplate the multiple, intersectional and, at times, competing truths of your life. The world is not stagnant, binary or black and white. Throw out the idea that it's one thing or another. BOTH/AND can build bridges where EITHER/OR sows division.

The truth is: people aren't either good or bad. We can be both agents of collective good and selfish or stuck in our ways. We can have both good intentions and poor follow-through. We can be both hopeful and realistic. To feel a full range of emotion is to hold many paradoxes. Learn to hold multiple narratives by listening to voices and opinions and people that are different from you. You will learn a lot by listening actively and reflecting to them what you hear. Making sure you hear what someone is saying requires reflective communication. After reflecting on what you hear, ask them, "Did I get that right?" or "Am I hearing you correctly?" This is how we bridge divides in communication.

There is never someone who is right and someone who is wrong. That binary isn't very helpful in building systems of collective care. In the same way that you are a complex, whole-ass human with joys and sorrows and regrets and flaws and things you can't control and things you can work harder on, so too is everyone else. We are all part of this complex, whole-ass thing together. As you learn to give yourself grace and see your own dignity, forgiveness and kindness and dignified actions for others become a whole lot easier.

When we look deeper into stories that are reduced to binaries like these, we find there are usually more twists, turns and complexity to the story. Look deeper into stories (ones you tell and ones you hear) that are reduced down to:

• Right or wrong

• Good or bad

• Broken or healed

• Heaven or hell

• Black or white

Investigate the messiness of being human. Look deeply into the uncertainty. Find nuance, subtlety, and dignity. Find that the world itself is a muddle of all things. Try embracing all things. Healing outside of these binaries is for everyone (literally). We all need to embrace our complex, intersecting, and ever-changing human nature.

When I made the choice to come out as non-binary and embrace a fluid gender expression, I was afraid to confront potential changes and losses that would inevitably come from this type of self-disclosure. Often, trans folks must choose between visibility and safety. I had been out as 'queer' and had openly shared my sexual orientation and queer relationships for nearly a decade, but I was so fearful to share that I was non-binary. I was known as a woman, and that simply didn't feel true any longer. In sharing the truth about my gender identity, I worried about many facets of my life: my work, my family of origin, my partnership, my health status and my access to safety, community and legal protections. Grief, loss and transformation have all been a part of my process coming into my non-binary identity. A deeper understanding of myself and my gender identity was discovered in my own therapy work under layers of lived experience, trauma and dissociation from my body. As I confront and work through these inner dynamics, I cultivate hope and self-love. Living outside of the binary and treating myself with acceptance and care have been the most powerful acts of self-compassion and liberation in my life. Choosing to share my transition, and my life outside of the gender binary is a choice born of freedom and joyful embodiment. Violence against trans and gender-non-conforming folks is real and anti-trans legislation and violence are at an all-time high. Choosing our truth, our joy, and our love is not simple. It is revolutionary.

It would be impossible for me to speak about living with intention without discussing my divorce from binaries. Rigid and all-or-nothing thought patterns are survival adaptations, not keys to healing and freedom. We have to investigate our belief systems, and shift our perspectives to hold real complexity and nuance in order to step into new ways of living.

One of my absolute favourite things about serving predominantly trans, non-binary, gender non-conforming folks and LGBTQIA+ people is watching them embrace self-knowing, fluidity, complexity and pride in their identities. These are innate parts of the queer experience, and they are also the things that save us. Queer love and resilience offer medicine to our world.

As we heal ourselves, our window of tolerance expands our access to more authenticity and aliveness. The main thing to understand about freeing yourself of any binary is that it expands your access to a wider spectrum of experience. This means that as you allow yourself to deepen into your grief, your capacity to access and feel joy also deepens. If you give up the roles of hero, villain, martyr or victim, can you find more complexity in those stories? What experiences have you been cutting yourself off from just because you are afraid they are not for you? Consider the binaries, the cages in your life you seek freedom from. Let curiosity, presence and complexity be your keys.

JOURNAL EXERCISE

• What stories (about yourself, others and the world) did you accept as facts in childhood?

....

....

....

....

• How have you redefined the truth as you have grown into a more complex position?

....

....

....

....

• What binaries, categories, or labels do you feel most constricted by?

....

....

....

....

WHAT BINARIES DO YOU FEEL MOST CONSTRICTED BY?

THE INNER HOME AND CORE BELIEF BLUEPRINTS

REPARENT YOUR INNER CHILD

THE BODY IS THE TEMPLE THAT HOUSES THE INNER FAMILY

The inner family entails your inner child, you (as the inner parent) and whomever else you call into your inner world for guidance and support. Your role in the inner family is to reparent your inner child, to heal their wounds and attune to what they need most. Your most adult self is the part of you that is most loving and responsible. You are the head of your inner family, you are the wise and present adult that you have been waiting for. No one is coming to save the parts of you that feel lost, insecure and uncertain; that is your job.

You are the perfect person to reparent your inner child. Your inner child is longing for your attention and care. This young and vulnerable part of you lives in the home inside you and is exposed to whatever you allow into your life through your thoughts, feelings and experiences. So frequently our inner child feels abandoned or neglected, like they grew up too fast.

Many of us, as children, didn't have adequate time and space to play, learn through our mistakes, express ourselves and be creative in the ways that we needed. Oftentimes, children will take on the failures of their environment or their caregivers. In clinical spheres, we call this "parentification" – parentified children take on responsibilities that they weren't prepared for growing up.

Parentification is a form of invisible childhood trauma that occurs when a child takes on roles of caregiver, mediator, emotional support or peacekeeper and is deprived of time to play. This cuts kids off from being kids – when children take on too much stress too fast, they become cut off from sources of play, expression, fun, and creativity.

As adults, we must learn how to connect with our inner child and attune to their needs in order to heal our inner child from the parentification they experienced. We must be a responsible leader of our inner family, and in doing so this allows the younger parts of us that were forced into stress and responsibility the opportunity to finally rest, and play, and be with ease.

Your inner child is not going anywhere and needs a loving, connected and attuned caregiver. Together, you can grieve the childhood you didn't have, find ways to welcome in joy and learn to prioritize your wants and needs.

There's always going to be a part of us that is sweet and creative, playful and wise. The inner child holds all these qualities while also being vulnerable and requiring your protection. You are the adult they have been waiting for, the one who understands everything they have been through.

WE MUST BE A
RESPONSIBLE
LEADER OF OUR
INNER FAMILY

CONNECTING WITH YOUR INNER CHILD

Here is a care practice for your inner child that you can use to soothe their worries and support with uncertainty. The best place to start with this practice is by checking in with your inner child. Notice when you have been feeling afraid, threatened, or easily stressed. Only connect with your inner child from a centred and grounded place. If you are upset or distressed, do something to calm yourself (refer to the various lists in this book and the self-care menu activities for ideas, page 76).

Sometimes a few breaths and adjusting your posture for the exercise is all that is needed to get centred. I like to breathe in through my nose and out through my mouth and repeat with each breath, "I'm here." Once you feel that you would be able to soothe a distressed child, you can move forward.

1   Light a candle and pause to breathe deeply.

2   Turn your attention inwards and notice how you feel.

3   Share your intention with your inner child. Talk to them out loud, using their name: "xxxx, I am here to listen and care for you."

4   Check in with the child in you. Ask them, "What are you going through?" Or "What do you need me to know?" Listen deeply.

5   Introduce them to yourself, catch them up to the current day. Tell them your name, your age and a little bit about your current life. Let them know you are a future version of themselves, tell them how you got through whatever was challenging for them. Recontextualize their experience.

6   Help your inner child understand what is going on in your life that is causing them to worry. Ask them if they are willing to put down some of the worry and trust you to take care of it, as the adult in their life that gets it.

7   Notice if they trust you and how it feels in your body when they let go of the worry. Know that trust is built over time so if this is the first time you are connecting with your inner child, it may take time to earn their trust.

8   Let your inner child know what you will do in your current life to make them a priority and that you will check back in with them soon. Tell them you love them, that they are special to you. Say "I am so glad you're here" and "This relationship matters to me".

Repeat this practice as often as needed.

OUR BELIEFS CREATE OUR THOUGHTS

CHILDHOOD STORIES

What did you internalise as true growing up? We all had stories that we were told, or that we told ourselves, in order to cope. Very often these childhood stories were warped versions of realities that we were shielded from or truths we were denied. Secrets and denial have a funny way of impacting the stories we tell as kids. These stories are a patchwork sewn together with assumptions and simplicity helping us to deal with the unknown. Kids are sponges, they soak up whatever juice their environment feeds them. They listen to everything and are sense-making machines.

CORE BELIEF CYCLE

Our inner beliefs are shaped by our experiences, and these beliefs can be explored to better understand certain difficulties and repeating patterns we face in our lives. This Core Belief Cycle Activity can be used to track where our beliefs come from, and how they influence our thoughts, feelings, actions and experiences.

Understanding the Cycle

Experiences > Beliefs > Thoughts > Feelings > Actions > Experiences

Our beliefs create our thoughts. Our thoughts include our ideas and opinions about ourselves, others and the world. Our thoughts make up our intentions and expectations. The inner chatter going on in our minds has a strong influence on the way we feel. Our feelings are powerful emotional messengers that communicate to us through complex body-based channels using neurotransmitters and hormones released by the brain and body. These emotional reactions can include feelings including fear, anger, sadness, joy, guilt, shame, love, disgust, surprise, and horror.

The way we manage our thoughts and feelings becomes our actions. Our behaviours, impulses and

THE CORE

BELIEF CYCLE

external reactions include the ways that we cope with difficult or dysregulated emotions. The way we act creates our experiences. Our experiences are how we relate and respond to moments and events in our life. These experiences can either confirm or contradict our beliefs.

The beliefs that we hold unconsciously have a not-so-subtle way of influencing the way we move through our lives. These core beliefs make up the way that we perceive ourselves, others, and the world around us. Frequently, these beliefs form in our early life and may be messages that we hear growing up that we internalise as 'truths'.

IDENTIFY YOUR CORE BELIEFS

Identifying your core beliefs starts by noticing themes and patterns in your thoughts, feelings, and experiences. You might notice patterns already in the ways that you relate to yourself and others.

Spend time reflecting on your inner wounds. The moments in your life that impacted the way you understood yourself in the world. Reflect on what went on for you during those deeply challenging experiences. What direction was your inner compass facing? You might notice your body carries a reaction, a stress response, when you hold these memories and wounds in your mind.

Go through the list of core beliefs that follows and read each of the negative statements out loud. Move through the entire list paying attention to your body and your felt sense as you recite these statements.

You may notice one or two of these statements affect you differently or hit home on a deeper, emotional level. Write these core beliefs down. Narrow your list down to no more than 3 core beliefs by repeating the statements and remaining mindful of your body's experience, letting your body wisdom guide you to the most central of the wounds needing healing.

For a full list of negative and positive beliefs and cognitions, and for a printable core belief tracker, visit intentionstherapy.com/print

Here are some negative core beliefs that may resonate with you:

• I am not good enough

• There is something wrong with me

• I am a failure / I can't do anything right

• I am a bad person

• I am a burden on everyone

• I don't deserve love

• I am worthless / I am inadequate

• I am different / I don't belong

• I did something wrong

• I cannot trust myself / I cannot trust my judgement

• It isn't safe to be myself

• I am in danger, I am not safe

CORE BELIEFS DRIVE OUR LIVES THROUGH OUR SUBCONSCIOUS

- I am permanently damaged

- The world is an unsafe place

- It is not okay to show my emotions

- I cannot stand up for myself

- I am helpless / I am powerless

- I have to be perfect / I must please everyone

- I can't trust others / people are malicious

- No one will love me / I have no one / I am alone

- The world is unfair / I am doomed

TRACK YOUR CORE BELIEF CYCLE

Now that you have identified 1-3 negative core beliefs that are operating subconsciously, it is your job to focus on these unhealed wounds with attention and intention.

Core beliefs drive our lives through our subconscious. When we are unaware of our fear-based beliefs, we have no choice but to continue the negative cycle they create.

The following guided process uses a printable core belief tracker that you can access at Intentionstherapy.com/print.

1   Start by listing the core beliefs that you have identified in the "belief" section.

2   Ask yourself, "what happened in my life that led me to believing this?" Your core beliefs come from the way you relate to yourself, others, and the world, based on your experiences. List relevant events in the "Experiences" section.

3   Now, turn to the "Thought" section, and list ideas, worries, opinions, expectations, and any thoughts relevant to the core belief you are working on. Your beliefs are the operating system for your thoughts.

4   The inner chatter in your mind directly impacts the way you feel. List your emotional state and internal reactions to these thoughts in the "Feelings" section. Don't hold back.

5   How do you act when you feel this way? List your behaviours, impulses, and external reactions in the "Actions" section.

6   Check back in with your experience. Look at the actions you have identified on your cycle – how are these actions serving you? What experiences are they creating? Are they simply confirming

your core belief and continuing the negative cycle?

7   Turn to the column on the left to unlock your
    negative cycle. The key to interrupting your core
    belief cycle is slowing down your external reactions
    and acting differently. List in the column on the left
    ways you can respond to the same thoughts and
    feelings with different, more aligned actions.

CHALLENGE YOUR NEGATIVE CORE BELIEFS

If you grew up believing you were not enough, and
couldn't do anything right, you would develop a
strong inner critic, judge yourself harshly, and feel
discouraged and frustrated. If you believe that you
are not enough, you act like you are not enough. Our
actions, and the way we show up for our life, work,
and relationships, directly create our experience.
So, if you believe and think and feel that you are not
enough, you will act that way, and your experiences
will confirm the belief that you are not enough.

The opposite is also true. If you act like you are worthy
of time and attention, you experience yourself as
being worthy.

If you are asking yourself how you can shift out of
your negative core belief systems, the answer is to
act differently.

It is up to you, which beliefs you want to be true about yourself. If you worry you are not a good friend, work on being a better friend and your friendships will transform. Imagine how a good friend would think, and feel, and act, and try out those positive ways of being. You don't have to do an impression of who you were yesterday. You can change if you want. You can be better if you want to. People make changes all the time.

How do I shift my core beliefs? The answer is to react differently.

SHIFT YOUR

CORE BELIEFS

The way you can interrupt any negative core belief cycle is by slowing down your external reactions, and responding in ways that are more aligned with yourself.

If we can notice our thoughts and feelings and consciously choose to act differently, our experiences will change.

Experiences that differ from our norm will challenge and contradict our negative beliefs. If you were convinced you were unloveable, you might be uncertain when good love arrives on your doorstep.

New, positive experiences can be uncomfortable if our negative core beliefs are deeply rooted.

If you are seeking relief from the current state of your life, you will need to make changes that differ from the way you have been moving through your life thus far. Healing requires openness to doing things differently, and trusting in new experiences. It is much easier to let go of what no longer serves us, when there are new experiences to reach for and grasp onto.

Change your actions and experiences, and your beliefs will transform.

WELCOME YOUR UNCERTAINTY HOME

If you want your life to change positively, you must deal with uncertainty.

Uncertainty is guaranteed when we are trying something new. So, as you embrace different experiences that challenge the negative core beliefs you learned early on, you may find yourself embarking down new paths with great uncertainty.

CHANGE YOUR ACTIONS AND EXPERIENCES AND YOUR BELIEFS WILL TRANSFORM

DO YOU GET LOST IN UNCERTAINTY?

Do you get lost in uncertainty? Do you fear the unknown, the future or the parts of life that are out of your control? You are not alone. Ask yourself, why have I learned to fear the unknown? What happened in my life that taught me that when I'm not in control, bad things happen?

Many people subscribe to a cultural narrative that uncertainty is intolerable. I find this mindset to be pessimistic on the surface but deeply rooted in expecting the worst from the world. This sounds like trauma to me. We can recognize this negative expectation and then choose to relate to the uncertainty differently. I like to remember that uncertainty is neutral, it is not always one thing or another.

RECALIBRATED VIEW OF UNCERTAINTY

In the unknown, there is mystery; in mystery, there is possibility, and with possibility, anything can happen. Here is the thing about life: there is so little we can control. Control isn't the point. To me, the point is to welcome it all.

Try and welcome the uncertainty you feel. Greet it as an unexpected guest who shows up after much travel. Notice how you can learn to trust yourself in the present, even in the face of the unknown. Practice this experiential exercise to self-soothe in the face of uncertainty.

EXPERIENTIAL EXERCISE: SOOTHING UNCERTAINTY WITH BREATH AND TOUCH

Before considering the uncertainty in your life, take a few moments to get centred with your breath.

Recite these affirmations as you inhale deeply and exhale fully:

Inhale: I Embrace myself in the here and now.

Exhale: I Release the impulse to be in control.

Inhale: I Embrace gratitude and openness to possibility.

Exhale: I Release fear and attachment to outcome.

Take a few more deep breaths, focusing on the rhythm of your breath.

Now, physically embrace yourself. Fold your arms around your body, positioning them in a way that feels natural and comfortable. You might try folding your arms across your stomach or just below your chest. Breathe deeply as you feel into this self-hug. You might find it comfortable to curve your hands around your sides.

Rest your hands on your shoulders or upper arm, wherever feels natural. Imagine the type of embrace you want from a close friend. Offer yourself a soft and soothing hug. Squeeze your arms with just enough pressure to create the sensation you are looking for. Offer yourself a light massage.

Feel free to rest your cheek on your hand or shoulder, rock back and forth and make any adjustments that deepen your self embrace. Hold the hug for as long as it feels good.

Recite aloud:

I am here.
I love myself.
I really really love myself!
I am open to the mysteries of my life.
I am willing to embrace the unknown in myself and my world.
I don't need to know everything to move forward, I learn by moving forward.

IN UNCERTAINTY THERE IS POSSIBILITY

JOURNAL EXERCISE

What expectations must I release in order to manage my discomfort with the unknown?

....

....

....

....

....

....

....

....

....

What could happen to my inner landscape if I welcomed uncertainty like it was a member of my inner family?

....

....

....

....

....

....

....

....

....

HUMAN CONNECTION: RELATIONSHIPS WITH THE SELF & OTHER

CONNECTION IS A NECESSITY FOR LIFE

THE RELATIONSHIP WITH SELF

Connection is a necessity for life.
Connection to self only deepens when we connect with others.
Connection with others only deepens when we connect with self.

The relationship you have with yourself is by far your longest and most important relationship you can cultivate. It may also be the coolest relationship you ever have, because you can steer it in any direction you choose.

The relationship with Self is the magnetic field powering your inner compass. Without this relationship, one is lost. Basing their life choices on the needs and whims of other people. Robbing themself of an opportunity to know their truest desires.

We don't get far when we are disconnected for long; we stagnate and our needs go unmet. When our needs go unmet, our body systems speak through symptoms. Physical and mental health symptoms, or feelings, are constantly communicating. Learning to understand what your symptoms are communicating is medicine. The medicine is simply speaking the language of your symptoms and tending accordingly.

If you learn to welcome and investigate your symptoms like they are a weary guest, you will tend to what is needed and heal the root of the distress.

REFLECT ON YOUR SYMPTOMS

1 Identify your most distressing and uncomfortable physical and mental symptoms in the last two weeks. Write them below:

....

....

....

....

....

....

2 Imagine you are running a fully staffed and operational bed and breakfast out of your home. You have a weary traveller arrive with the symptoms listed above.

....

....

....

....

....

....

3 Using the resources at your disposal, what
   recommendations would you give this traveller?
   Do they need a warm meal, a glass of water and
   a good night's sleep? Do they need to ice their
   injuries, elevate their feet, and take the load off?

....
....
....
....
....
....

4 Write your recommendations for this traveller and
   heed your own advice in the next 24 hours.

....
....
....
....
....
....

You don't have to be a doctor or a medical
professional to advise someone to tend to themselves.
In this case, that someone is yourself.
Rest easy, my dear.

HUMAN CONNECTION: RELATIONSHIPS WITH OTHER HUMANS

Let me highlight for you the importance of feeling seen and heard. Emotions are physical and neurological responses in our body that are meant to have a beginning, middle and end. The reason why many seek therapy is because they feel dysregulated in their emotional responses. They feel "stuck" in a stress response, they feel chronic fear or sadness or irritability or disconnect and they are unable to resolve their emotions.

Emotions are tunnels, or portals we must pass through. Essentially, we must feel the emotion so it can pass. If we don't feel our feelings, they get stuck.

Therapy allows people to work through their emotional tunnels with support. Feeling safe to process complex emotions or chronic stress is the priority of therapy. Therapists are trained to attune to client experiences of pain and discomfort. When we live with unresolved stress and emotion, it wears on our minds and bodies. We get "stuck in the tunnel" when we are not able to feel and release our emotions and return back to safety and connection. Ask yourself – Am I working through my pain or getting stuck in suffering?

We are able to soothe ourselves and return to connection when we feel seen and heard, which only happens through connection. Humans need one another to live and connect and feel. We need one another's help in feeling our way through the world.

WE NEED ALL OF US:
NO ONE IS DISPOSABLE
WE NEED ALL OF YOU:
NO PART OF YOU IS DISPOSABLE

We need one another. I need you as desperately as you need me. No parts of humanity are bad, or wrong, or flawed. We need all of us; all of the complexity and individual uniqueness and diversity is needed to establish community. Our world is in desperate need of your unique voice and gifts, no part of you can be left out or left behind. You are not alone on this journey inwards and towards what you desire. Intentional Living is connected living. Connecting with our relationships and the world around us becomes easier when we can comfortably connect inwards with ourselves.

The further inwards we go, the more access we have to the powerful healing potential of darkness, and our love of self deepens. Think of your inner world as a cocoon you must retreat to in order to grow your wings. No freedom without intention. No intention without loving connection. Let your curiosity about the truth carry you through the unknown. Trust that

NO FREEDOM WITHOUT INTENT

the energy of your life will sustain you, and gravity will hold you to the Earth.

Trust that you are part of something massive. Trust that you are thoroughly interconnected with everything and everyone around you. Trust that you are here for a reason. Maybe this life is a gift that can be shared. Trust that this perfect cocktail of biology + identity + family + lived experience makes your life unique and special and worth living.

It is our own personal responsibility to heal our relationship with self, unlearn patterns of fear, and embrace our dignity through compassionate connection. It is our own responsibility to crawl into the unknown, the darkness of our inner world, and look into our shadows. As we take responsibility for how we feel, we heal. As we heal, we liberate ourselves from fear. In freedom, we can access authenticity, expansion, peace, creativity, and aliveness.

I believe that healing the relationship with self is an act of collective resistance. Speaking from my lived experience as a queer, trans, neurodivergent individual, repairing my relationship with myself has refreshed my capacity to show up in whole, empowered ways for my relationships and my community. I know that my well-being and liberation are inextricably linked to the liberation of my neighbours.

Humans need one another to survive. Humans need healthy and whole relationships. Relationships with self and others are survival necessities. No one can be left behind.

ACTIVITY SUGGESTION

Are you looking for connection? Find a local barbershop or hairdresser and get your hair cut or reach out to a local beauty parlour or nail salon and enjoy a treatment of your choice.

Not into a personal service? Visit a local library, coffee shop, bookstore or diner. I promise you will witness community and human connection.

PRACTICE LOVE, AND UNLEARN THE WAYS OF UN-LOVING.

Love is an undercurrent that is always present. Practicing Love is like practicing gratitude, enjoyment, acceptance, connection, celebration, and fun. These frequencies just need to be tuned into, and the possibilities are endless. I promise practicing love will increase your vibration and help you to find harmony and success.

PRACTICING LOVE WILL HELP YOU FIND HARMONY AND SUCCESS

What human connections and demonstrations of love have lifted my spirit?

....

....

....

What relationships have wounded or hurt me?

....

....

....

Through these wounds, what did I learn about myself, and my relational needs?

....

....

....

What relationships have opened me up to new possibilities and hopes for myself?

....

....

....

ACTIVITY
LOVE LETTER CHAINS

Few words can describe the joy a written letter can bring to someone who is longing for connection, and their voice to be heard.

Who do you know that might need some love? A long-distance friend? A neighbour you see walking their dog? Someone who needs a reminder of your care?

Write them a love letter and send it their way. You may even find yourself a new pen pal.

Love letter chains are a simple way to share the love.

1   Write your letter and express yourself!

2   Ask the recipient of your letter to share this love by paying it forward.

3   Tuck a "love letter chains" slip into your note before sending it.

To print a "love letter chains" message, go to intentionstherapy.com/print

THE NECESSITY OF TIME, SPACE, AND PLACE FOR HUMAN CONNECTION.

Humans require actual space to connect: space is a combination of time and place.

The ever-expanding internet, phones, and technology like social media have increased the quantity of human connection. Virtual and long-distance connection is a form of human connection. I will not discount connections sustained online, especially not in the digital age where so many of us are needing to connect across divides of time, place and culture to find unity in our isolation.

In a time of ongoing pandemic, we have been enduring many plagues that perpetuate isolation and loneliness. Necessary spaces for human connection, replenishment, and gathering, have been limited, or lost altogether in the need for quarantine, and limitations to in-person gatherings due to public health risk.

This all being said, the reality that humans require this Earth in order to connect does not just go away, because we are in a time of the plague. We still need space. We still need time together in shared places.

We still need one another. We still need spaces to gather and connect. We still need community. We need places to be ourselves with one another.

We need spaces for meaning making, reflection, and process. We need art, culture, togetherness, ritual. We need healing spaces. Places to gather and feel. Places to exchange energy with aligned humans. Places to be in spirit together.

Our collective well-being requires the preservation of spaces where people gather to feel and exist with one another.

In these times of physical sickness and spiritual ailment, isolation abounds.

In order to thrive, humans require places that host:

• Celebration

• Remembrance

• Togetherness

• Connection

• Repair

• Transformation

• Loving Care

Where do you find time and space to connect meaningfully?

THE PORTAL INWARD: THE BROKEN PLACE WHERE THE LIGHT GETS IN

All humans have a spirit. All humans on this Earth have a spiritual and emotional and healing-based field of energy that can be injured by our connections. Human connection is a necessity in this life. Connection can be both a space of pain and love. There is no suffering without connection and there's no connection without suffering. No mud, no lotus.

In order to find the rose amidst the thorns, we must find a portal inward. The portal inward is the broken place where you allow light to enter. The portal inward is usually a wound or relational injury. They are not problems; they are portals we can travel through to heal.

I don't know any healing human who doesn't talk about their relationships with self and other. Our relationships are the source of most of our suffering. Our suffering lets us know we are connected and alive. The greatest gift I can offer anyone I love is my presence, and space for them to suffer. My offering of presence and space serves as a portal inward for my clients and loved ones.

ALL HUMANS HAVE A SPIRIT

Thich Nhat Hanh offers 4 statements to communicate true presence to those we love:

1   My darling, I am here for you.

2   I know you are there, and I am very happy.

3   Darling, I know you suffer. That is why I am here for you.

4   Darling, I suffer, please help.

There is healing power in suffering. There is magic potential in darkness. There is value to our suffering in connection. There is a deep necessity that we all have to move inward for transformation. To look at our wounds and our shadows and offer presence. One does not just become a butterfly. You must go into a dark cocoon to let go and rest, and that cocoon is a deep generative space for something new to be reborn. This is the work of Intentions. You must move inward into your own inner darkness to clarify what is needing to transform in your life. You have to look inward, offer presence and space to suffer. You must feel your pain, bring your injuries to light, take time and space to shed and grieve. Only then can you imagine a new life. Only then can you spread your wings and move towards what you desire.

MY PORTAL INWARD, MY SPIRITUAL WOUND

"What are your special intentions?" This might seem like a strange question to ask a child, but it was something I was asked every day growing up.

Every night before bed, I would gather with my family. My three sisters, my parents, and I would join together in our home for prayer. My dad would ask, "What would you like to pray for?" and we would pause to identify our intentions. We would go one person at a time, and we would list our intentions behind our prayers, and then we would recite our prayers together.

In childhood, my answer to this question changed every night, depending on my needs. The intentions I set might have sounded something like this:

> "My special intentions are for the people hit by the last hurricane and anyone who is homeless tonight. I want to pray for Grandpa to get well soon and for my family and friends to be happy and healthy. I'm worried about my test this week, so I want to pray for confidence as I study."

These were my special prayers, the messages I wanted to lift up to God.

I was born into a devout Catholic family of six. My family was very involved in our local parish. My mother and father had my oldest sister just 18 months before my twin sister and I were born. Four years later, my youngest sister joined the Sullivan family.

My parents are kind and loving people. My mom is someone who has allowed me to witness the depth of her faith, and my dad is a generous man and a fantastic listener. I was never abused or neglected by my parents. Even during my rocky transition into adulthood, I knew I could rely on my family to be a safety net to minimize any setbacks I faced. Regardless of our differing politics and beliefs, I could rely on my parents for help during bouts of serious illness, housing crisis, job loss, or death of a loved one. My parents were my safety net when I fell, and the scaffold that allowed me to reach new heights. For this, I am deeply humbled and immensely grateful. I am privileged to have kind and loving parents, but I know this is not a universal experience.

My parents taught my sisters and I discipline and self-control. We all had a decent grasp on what was "right" and what was "wrong" in terms of behaviour and communication, and our parents helped us to learn from our mistakes.

As we grew into ourselves throughout childhood and as emerging adults, we each developed our own sense of self-discipline. Discipline of self and the ability to speak the language of our needs were the basis of our individual freedom.

AN UPBRINGING OF FAITH

We were a beautiful, Catholic family.
We still are a beautiful, diverse family.

As all of us grew up, we individuated. My family became more diverse as we all aged into the truths about ourselves. We shed certain identities, and picked up different ways of understanding ourselves. Our beliefs and perspectives changed. They are still changing, shaped by our truth. Shaped by our lives.

Every night, we would pray "Our Father", "Hail Mary," and "Glory Be". The richness and beauty of this bedtime prayer ritual infused our daily life. We would pray before every meal, and in school, we started each class with a prayer. Growing up, prayer was a simple and efficient part of my daily routine. Prayer satisfied so many of my needs into one. My family would gather every night and set intentions.

Even when the culture of the Catholic Church started to hurt me more than love me, prayer was where I found connection, meaning, and support. I believe intention is at the root of prayer. So turning inwards to seek guidance, clarity, and purpose in a world that told me I was a sinner became a natural way to survive.

Existing as a visibly queer individual in many evangelical Christian traditions means exposure to the insidious trauma of minority stress. This is why so many LGBTQIA+ folks are late to bloom into their identities. We moved inwards for survival. We learn early that true expressions of self are dangerous, and we cut ourselves off from the truths that pose a threat to our survival. So you can imagine how someone raised Catholic who is also queer could be wounded and ostracized by their organized religion and its community of followers even before they found out they were queer.

My religious trauma hosts some of my deepest wounds. My religious trauma is my most potent portal inward, the most fertile inner space for me to plant seeds of hope and restorative justice. So many queer individuals hold spiritual trauma in their body; we hold fear, confusion, dysphoria, and rage. I grieve the years I lost to hating myself, seeing nothing but darkness and sin in the mirror. I mourn my loss of faith, my loss of connection to divinity. I grieve for my queer, trans, and non-binary siblings who have endured pervasive psychological injury from religious messages, communities, and experiences.

Here is the good news: adaptive spirituality is beautiful. Some of my most potent rituals emerge only in the shadows. So many of the queer folks I know who are healing from spiritual erasure, minority stress, and psychological trauma have emerged with a more nuanced, intersectional, and integrative faith.

There is goodness still here, look into the darkness and see for yourself.

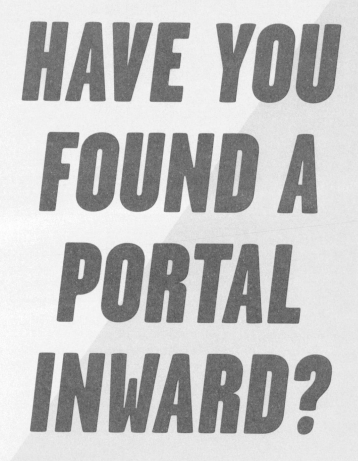

JOURNAL EXERCISE

• What helpful rituals and practices helped you
  to survive or cope with your upbringing?

....

....

....

....

• Were there any threats that caused you to delay
  self-expression or move inwards for survival?

....

....

....

....

....

• Have you found a portal inward? Which wounds
  and injuries are you willing to work through to
  heal your spirit?

....

....

....

....

FINDING YOUR PORTAL INWARD

How do you get in touch with your Spirit?

My answer: Find ways to be with the mysteries of your life.

When being asked how we can connect with our spirit, I think the simplest answer I can offer comes from my own experience. For so long after I stopped practising Catholicism, I continued to sit in silence and meditate on the mysteries of my own life. I called what I was doing meditation.

To find the portal inward requires us to look for the sacred divinity within ourselves.

I promise you, if you sit in silence for long enough, mysteries will come to you.

What does your spirit need the most at this point in your healing?

....

....

....

Ways I connect with my spirit, or life energy:

....

....

Examples:

• Silence

• Meditation

• Breathwork

• Prayer

• Music

• Journaling

• Movement

• Nature

• Connection

• Sound

• Experience

• Dance

LET LOVE RESET YOUR INNER COMPASS

As an emerging queer adult in conservative Catholic communities, I was exposed to some stark contrast. My inner compass was spinning with personal and moral questions of which I had no answer. My previously reliable North and South poles began to blur. Figuring out my needs, my desires, and my aim became more challenging, and I started to really question who I was.

My queerness, my gender and sexuality, was something so vague and blurry, I didn't even know what it was. It took another few years to work through my own denial of these feelings, but by the time I was 16 someone had caught my eye in the breezeway of my high school.

This person was not a man. Not only that, but they actually seemed interested in me! And, oh no, they might be flirting? Cue gay panic.

I had fallen in love; why did it feel like an identity crisis?

When I consider the landscape of our school and the utter lack of visibility and spaces for LGBTQ safety, the panic makes sense. I send so much love to high

MY INNER COMPASS WAS SPINNING

I SET MY INTENTION TO BE AS HONEST WITH MYSELF AS I COULD

school Dani. I want to tell them, "Love is good. Queer love can be magic. But stay safe, little one, the road to your truth is long and winding. You don't need to rush or have it all figured out."

Who would have thought having a high school sweetheart would bring up so much pain and conflict? The only thing that helped me to anchor into a place of hope was intention. I knew my inner compass would continue to spin unless I re-established my aim. Was it more important for me to remain open to love or to comply with cultural norms?

I set my intention to keep my heart open to love, no matter the wreckage.

I set my intention to be as honest with myself as I could.

I told my terrified heart, "it's okay to want what you want."

JOURNAL EXERCISE

- How has falling in love, with something or someone, changed your perspective on your life?

....

....

- Has love, desire, or longing for something different ever changed the course of your life? How can you let love reset your inner compass?

....

....

THE TOWER

CRUMBLES

THE TOWER CRUMBLES TO LET IN LIGHT

The Tower tarot card carries the meaning of sudden change, destruction, chaos and awakening. It is an image that helps us to understand the destruction that is needed to transform. The crumbling tower symbolizes the tearing down of harmful structures or false perceptions.

The Tower is a symbol of power and reminds me of the dominant narratives running our mind, and our world. Portrayed on the tarot card, The Tower is being struck by a bolt of lightning and depicts sudden awareness and destruction of ignorance. It symbolizes a sudden revelation or a new piece of truth that turns your life on its head.

Aside from falling in love, there was one lightning bolt that brought my relationship to my faith down as a teenager: I lost a grandparent to suicide. This event sent my relationship with myself into a state of chaotic questioning. I was totally unprepared for the life-shattering unknown that myself and my family faced. It felt like the tower I had been living in and co-constructing for 16 years had crumbled to the ground. The Earth cracked open beneath me and threatened to swallow me whole. I was filled with every emotion possible, in a constant flux and at a high intensity.

This grief reset my life. Allowing myself to feel the depths of this loss and really let it affect my heart has changed the direction of my life. Any earth-shattering experience will force you to re-evaluate your inner compass. Allowing these experiences to change us, to soften our hearts, is the most valuable lesson in love.

Let your pain, your suffering, and your losses break you open. Let them tear down everything you thought you knew about life and death. It's okay if it takes a lifetime to build something new. The tower crumbles to let light in.

Over a decade later, and my family is still doing the work to build our lives back in the wake of such profound loss. For my family, learning to grieve needed to be something we did together as much as we did on our own.

The mystery of my grandmother's death was never resolved. I still grieve her loss and grapple with the truth about what happened. The grief is how I continue to hold her in my heart – I am not looking to resolve this mystery. Sometimes the mystery is what generates light. Not knowing, not being able to land on any solid conclusions to my questions allowed me to continue to look into my wounding with love. Let your deepest wounds be portals you carry your inner family through with love.

LET YOUR PAIN AND SUFFERING BREAK YOU OPEN

JOURNAL EXERCISE

- What did you learn about pain, death and suffering through your family's collective experience?

....

....

....

- Did you have to take space from your family of origin to learn more about yourself?

....

....

....

- What sudden realization has felt earth-shattering but led to transformation in your life?

....

....

....

- What helped you to overcome the hardships and deal with change?

....

....

....

WHAT HELPED YOU OVERCOME HARDSHIPS AND DEAL WITH CHANGE?

GRIEF
MEDICINE

I WANTED ANSWERS TO EVERY MYSTERY I FACED

MAGIC FOR A SEARCHING HEART

When my life was turned on its head by both loss and love, I needed answers. My mental health began to slip and I struggled deeply with depression, severe anxiety and panic attacks. I wanted answers to every mystery I faced. I wanted certainty when none could be found in my trauma.

I would read whatever spiritual texts I could get my hands on, regardless of tradition or origin. My favourite part of doing religious research is finding threads of truth and similarity woven through each religious tradition or experience. In college, I lived in Chicago, Illinois. While studying at Loyola, I majored in Advocacy and Social Change in the School of Communication. I concentrated most of my studies on peace and conflict in interfaith settings. I worked for half a decade for a non-profit called "Interfaith Worker Justice" preaching the truth that 'all religions believe in justice'. I dove deeply into learning Buddhist philosophy and teachings, practising Yoga and Ayurvedic traditions, researching interfaith conflict and collaboration, finding my roots as a green witch, leaning into Earth magic and astrology, researching the Bahá'í faith through ethnography, and learning about spiritual practices from all over the world.

So, why was I researching religious tradition and interfaith peace making? Why was I obsessed with conflicts and war fought in the name of God? What was I truly seeking? Answers to questions my heart was asking but couldn't find words for. I was looking for my truth, searching for my inner north. I knew what my family wanted me to believe. I knew what my teachers wanted me to believe, but what did I actually hold to be true at my core?

The silence inside me, the lack of an answer, was terrifying. If I didn't want to feel the fear of not knowing, I could just keep searching.

Intense spiritual research and near-constant questioning of my own beliefs helped me deal with the change and uncertainty that filled my teens and early 20s. My research satiated my desire for control and meaning and helped me to cope with the realities of my family's loss and my own spiritual wounding. Looking to many different religious texts and spiritual practices, I found my own way through the darkness and grief.

Doing these intellectual and spiritual deep dives allowed me to swim to greater depths in my own inner landscape. In my exploration, I realized that within any dark moment lies the potential for change.

Grief is pain + love. So, if you are in pain, and loss feels everywhere, know that this pain is evidence of love. You are allowed to hurt, allowed to care. There is no being human without loss and the hurt parts show us what we love.

Grief is medicine – as we move through it, we heal. If you resist being affected by your grief, your body holds onto fear and constriction. The resistance of grief is traumatic for our body, our spirit, and our relationships. Understanding and experiencing our grief is the antidote to trauma.

Grief heals our losses with intention.

Grief is how the living continue to honour the dead.

People with religious trauma need love.
People with psychological wounding need magic.
People with spiritual loss need to understand that life and death are still here.
Life is still sacred and fragile.

Life and Death hold us with love. These forces are human and natural and a big part of what we're here to experience. If we can experience life and death with love, they are profound teachers.

Grief is soft and gentle medicine. Grief is the love we need, the magic that unites life and death. A complex embodied emotional experience that requires our attention. Grief is not the wound, but the medicine that heals our wounds as we suffer.

Grief is something that we need to experience – it's not something that we can just think about, we have to actually feel it. This is something that the Catholic faith gave me: spaces and practices to access grief. Grief can be ritualized; it can be celebrated. There are ways that we can hold time and space, to feel grief and to move through all of the different expressions of our loss:

• Light a candle and play a song that helps you remember.

• Look at pictures, make a collage or scrapbook honouring your losses.

• Share stories, reflect, journal and reminisce.

GRIEF CAN BE RITUALIZED; IT CAN BE CELEBRATED

JOURNAL EXERCISE

• How did your family and culture process loss and honour death and grief?

....

....

....

....

....

• What practices have helped you to remember what you love?

....

....

....

....

....

• How have you learned to care for your body, mind and spirit in the wake of loss and change?

....

....

....

....

....

FINDING HOPE IN MYSTERY

LEARN THE SACRED ART OF HOPING

My heart swirls with the mystery of being alive. Sometimes, these mysteries are challenging to befriend, and darkness abounds. We must learn the sacred art of hoping. Looking into our questions and uncertainty for light, inspiration and wisdom.

I have always been passionate about figuring out the invisible forces that shape our world. I have always found magic, God even, in nature and in connection. I think this is because many of the barriers to divinity were removed for me and God was made accessible to me through my parents, my home environment, the schools I attended and the people around me who showed me love.

This hopefulness is a privilege my ancestors gave me - something unearned, but a gift nonetheless. I benefited greatly from the faith and traditions of those who came before me. I was taught prayers, by my parents and family, like scripts that helped me learn how to talk to God. I learned to connect with the divine in me and all around me, whenever I set an intention.

Finding hope, and connecting with sources of divinity, magic and life itself is something we all have the capacity for. We can all access goodness, hope, and light.

Having witnessed and brought care to my own spiritual wounding, I want to share a story with you of my recent return to prayer.

THE JOYFUL MYSTERIES

I am 27, holding hands with my wife, Alexa, on the last day of our honeymoon. We are sitting in front of a fire that I built on a week-long trip to Tully Pond, a small freshwater lake at the foot of Tully Mountain in rural Orange, Massachusetts. We wanted to spend our honeymoon in nature, surrounded by the changing autumn leaves.

The afternoon prior, we picked red apples and Alexa made cinnamon apple pancakes to eat by the fire on our last morning. We'd just loaded up our rental car and were waiting out our check-out time by the fire.

My wife was raised in a Jewish-American family with roots in Brooklyn, New York and Georgia. We had just gotten married by the Atlantic Ocean and celebrated in my parents' backyard with our closest family and friends.

I asked my wife if she would be willing to pray the Rosary with me. She said, "I would be happy to, but I have never prayed it before." I let her know she was in good company and that I was a little rusty myself – the last time I prayed the Rosary, I was in middle school.

My relationship to prayer, spirituality and ritual has totally transformed since my middle-school days. I remember joining my three sisters and mother outside the parish chapel before school to pray the Rosary. We would gather around a statue of the Sacred Mother and speak our intentions directly to Holy Mary, the mother of Jesus. The Rosary contains many prayers and to follow the beads for one round requires reciting over 65 prayers. This powerful offering takes about 20 minutes to pray while you meditate on the mysteries of Jesus's life.

Using a Rosary bought in my late teens on a trip to the Vatican, my wife and I joined hands. There was so much energy in the moment, it got caught in my throat and I felt my eyes welling. Never did I think I would have it in me to pray the Rosary again. I was afraid I had lost touch, and I felt so angry and rejected by the church for so many years. My spirit was so wounded; why did I want to sit with my wife and pray this prayer by a campfire?

Life carries mystery and our love is fresh. I needed to honour this transition from independence into union by remembering my connection with life and death. I remembered my portal inward and allowed myself to backtrack towards a faith tradition that wounded me. This time, I had new ways of being; this time, I knew the truth: that I was welcome to connect with divinity, if that was my choice.

I imagined my middle school self, joining my wife and me by the fire and snacking on pancakes with fresh apples. I left an opening for this younger version of self to sit next to me. A space for them to witness my return to prayer.

In front of Tully Pond, my fingers fumbled with the Rosary beads, my voice quivered with the cold morning. We prayed while meditating on joyful mysteries.

Sitting with my wife. Wearing three layers of sweaters and sharing a blanket by the fire. The crisp morning air was still. No answers, only questions.

We set intentions for our love and began to pray.

WE SET INTENTIONS

FOR OUR LOVE

JOURNAL EXERCISE

- How have you learned to embrace joy in the mystery and uncertainty?

....

....

- What intentions would you like to carry forward?

....

....

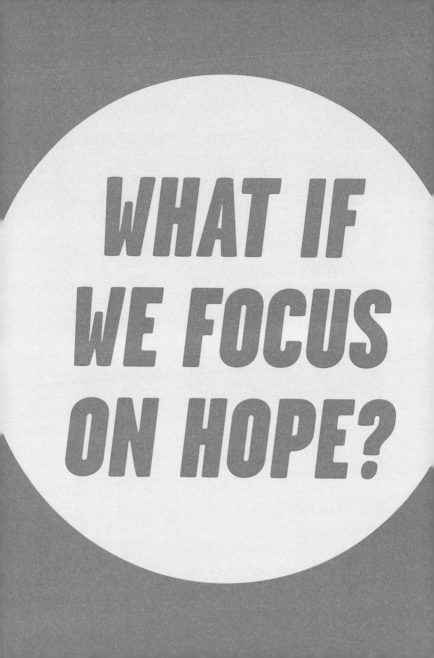

A CASE FOR HOPE

What if we focus on hope?

What if we spent equal time imagining a positive future as we do worrying about the unknown?

There is hope.

We can hope.

Hope resides here, in the present.

Hoping is a practice.

If you aren't spiritual or have little experience with prayer, but you want to uplift your spirit and feel better, practice hope.

Hope is an action. It requires connecting with our desires.

Hope is a reimagining of our path.

Hope is connection with desire; it is intention in action.

Hope is a practice that helps orient your inner compass.

Hope is a feeling. You can't practice hope without feeling.

Feeling the longing and excitement and joy in simply

expecting the best for yourself, your family, your world.

Hope requires we experience yearning.

Hope is about witnessing your dreams, really feeling into your dreams, before they come to fruition.

Hoping is a powerful exercise in self-trust.

So, let me ask you again, what is the worst that can happen if you were to focus on hope? What might happen, if before you picked up your phone in the morning, you spent 60 seconds considering what you hope for your day?

I try to live my life with as little urgency as possible, and I strongly urge you to look for hope in your life. This is a vital practice that the world needs to embrace.

Look for hope by imagining a future with 5 per cent more ease, 2 per cent more connection, 1 per cent more intention.

You don't have to do a 180 in order to find the good in your life. You might just need to open your eyes, or shift your view. You don't need to find 100 per cent more love in order to feel good.

What would it be like if you had just 1 per cent more love? How would that feel in your life? What direction might you turn for it?

I promise that looking for hope won't require you to change drastically or search for very long. Incremental gains and small shifts really do build up.

Despair is easy to fall into, and endless.

Hope is simple to find, and endless as well.

The possibility of change is real. People heal all the time. People get better. There is hope for all of us.

HOPING IS A POWERFUL EXERCISE IN SELF-TRUST

LETTER TO SELF OF HOPEFUL INTENTION

As you finish your journey with this text, write yourself
a letter to read the next time you go searching for
meaning. Write to your future self, sharing your hopes.
Share in colourful detail exactly what you imagine.
Describe the connections you will make and the
experiences you will be present for.

....
....
....
....
....
....
....
....
....
....
....
....
....
....
....
....
....
....
....

....

....

....

....

....

....

....

....

....

....

....

....

....

Set clear, heartfelt intentions for yourself, your life, your world. Trust yourself to bring these hopes to your world.

It is my hope that this book helps you with the mysteries you carry. Thank you so much for your work, here, on yourself. Thank you for setting hopeful intentions, and bringing darkness to light. I am so glad you exist.

Much love to you,

Dani Sullivan

FURTHER READING

Learn More About Self-Healing and Collective Care:

- Self-Healing Articles & Intentional Resources –
  Dani Sullivan, LCSW – intentionstherapy.com

- Rest Is Resistance: A Manifesto – Tricia Hersey (Founder of The Nap
  Ministry)

- Pleasure Activism – Adrienne Marie Brown

- Healing Through Words – Rupi Kaur

- Untamed – Glennon Doyle (and the We Can Do Hard Things podcast)

- No Bad Parts: Healing Trauma and Restoring Wholeness with Internal
  Family Systems –
  Richard Schwartz, PhD

- Fucking Magic – Clementine Morrigan (and the Fucking Cancelled
  Podcast)

- Lessons in Liberation: An Abolitionist Toolkit for Educators – Bettina
  L. Love, Jay Gillen, and
  Mariame Kaba

Learn More About Spirituality:

- Love Letter to the Earth, No Mud, No Lotus –
  Tich Naht Hahn

- Be Here Now – Baba Ram Dass (and Going Home documentary)

- All Men Are Brothers, Non-Violent Resistance – Mahatma Gandhi

- When Women Were Birds: 54 Variations on Voicie – Terry Tempest
  Williams

- No Future without Without Forgiveness –
  Desmond Tutu

- The Rhythm of Life – Living Every Day with Passion and Purpose –
  Matthew Kelly

- The Green Witch – Arin Murphy-Hiscock

- Radical Acceptance, Radical Compassion,
  the Self-Acceptance Project – Tara Brach

Learn More About Queer Experience and Gender

- Beyond the Gender Binary – Alok V. Menon
- Undoing Gender – Judith Butler
- Sister Outsider: Essays and Speeches – Audre Lorde
- All About Love: New Visions –bell hooks
- Come as You Are – Emily Nagoski
- Living in this Queer Body podcast – Asher Pandjiris

Learn More About Neurodiversity and Mental Health

- NeuroQueer Heresies – Dr Nick Walker
- Unmasking Autism, Laziness Does Not Exist – Dr. Devon Price
- The "Really Strange Boxset" Explores Anxiety, Trauma, Pain and Touch – Steve Haines
- Demystifying Disability – Emily Ladau
- Neurodivergent Friendly Workbook of DBT Skills – Sonny Jane Wise
- Supporting Transgender and Autistic Youth and Adults – Finn Gratton, LMFT

The Author's Favourite Books and Tools:

- Ayurveda: The Science of Self-Healing – Vasant Lad
- You Were Born for This: Astrology for Radical Self-Acceptance – Chani Nicholas, and the CHANI Astrology App
- Queer Tarot – An Inclusive Deck and Guidebook – Ashley Molesso and Chess Needham
- Atlas of the Heart, The Gifts of Imperfection, Dare to Lead – Breneé Brown (and the Unlocking Us podcast)
- Birdwatching for Your Mental Health! E-Birds App by Cornell Lab of Ornithology
- Guided Meditations from Headspace, Calm and tarabrach.com

A THANK YOU

To my wife –

Thank you for showing me a life I didn't know I deserved and for painting our world in colours I didn't know existed. I am madly in love with you.

To my beautiful, diverse family –

Thank you for teaching me how to build a life and for providing me with a solid foundation. Relationships with you have healed my soul.

To humanity, the human family –

Thank you for teaching me that the best things in life are a muddled mess of every colour on the spectrum. This is my love letter to you.

To you –

Thank you for existing. It is my hope that this book helps you with the mysteries, the uncertainty and the darkness you carry. I am so glad you are here.

Dani Sullivan, LCSW, is an educator, clinical social worker and the founder of Intentions Therapy. They have worked as a macro social worker, focusing on community advocacy and organizing for social change. They established the Intentions Therapy Practice in 2020, since using an interdisciplinary approach to offer a space for self-inquiry, exploration, and healing. This is their first book.

A gift for you

Enjoy your gift.